LOST BRIGHTON

CHRISTOPHER HORLOCK

AMBERLEY

Acknowledgements

Most of the photographs are from my own collection, but several come from other local historians and collectors, to whom grateful thanks are due. Robert Jeeves, of 'Step Back in Time', Queen's Road, has allowed a number of his postcard views to appear, as has fellow collector Peter Booth. Photographs from the James Gray Collection are courtesy of the Regency Society. Other images come from Margaret Taylor, Malcolm Dawes, Philippe Garner, Mick Thatcher and *The Argus* newspaper. Help with dates and various facts and figures came from Trevor Cox, Douglas d'Enno, Peter Hill, Laurie Marshall and Trevor Povey. The Keep archival centre at Moulsecoomb provided numerous resources, particularly period newspapers and street directories.

First published 2019

Amberley Publishing
The Hill, Stroud
Gloucestershire, GL5 4EP

www.amberley-books.com

British Library Cataloguing in Publication Data.

A catalogue record for this book is available from the British Library.

ISBN 978 1 4456 8956 2 (print)
ISBN 978 1 4456 8957 9 (ebook)

Origination by Amberley Publishing.
Printed in the UK.

Contents

Introduction

Brighton has changed out of all recognition since the Second World War. Much-loved amenities have been lost, little of architectural importance has been built and huge areas redeveloped with box-like buildings rendering them sterile and characterless. Its past amenities and attractions were extraordinary, and if Brighton seems busy today, it's nothing compared to how it was in the past, particularly in the years between the wars.

The city has attracted visitors for some 300 years. They first came in the 1730s, mainly for health reasons. Wealthy individuals who were ill were quick to respond to the 'seawater cure', which physicians were promoting to treat virtually every ailment of the day, and Brighton, a stagecoach journey away from London, was ideally located to serve their needs. The subsequent provision of hotels, ballrooms, bath buildings, theatres and racecourse, which would now be termed 'resort facilities', can be seen as the genesis of the pleasure town Brighton would become.

Holiday crowds, 1931.

The visits (from 1783) and eventual residency of George, Prince of Wales (later George IV) gave enormous impetus to the development of the town during the early 1800s, with many new streets, squares and crescents expanding the town's boundaries. Much of Brighton's finest architecture was built at this time. The coming of the railway in 1841 saw a further mushrooming of amenities and topographical expansion, which continued into the Victorian and Edwardian periods. Between the wars, Brighton reached the height of its seaside holiday popularity, but then, as with other resorts, its attraction declined as a place for a week or fortnight's stay, with trips abroad becoming cheaper and other forms of holiday taking over. Brighton responded with new initiatives to gain visitors and trade. Conferences became big business, with the Metropole Hotel first to lay on purpose-built facilities to accommodate large-scale meetings and exhibitions. With the 1960s came the town's first high-rise flats, the Churchill Square shopping complex and plans for Brighton Marina. Many streets of housing were swept away during this period, a substantial number of which could have been retained if modernised. A second Churchill Square was only just averted in the North Laine area.

Brighton and neighbouring Hove combined as one administrative authority in 1987. City status was granted in 2000 and the town once known as just Brighton became the city of Brighton and Hove. Since then, while its many students and younger inhabitants remain buoyant about life in Brighton, the resort is sliding into a period of decline, with many concerns to address, such as housing, street sleepers, traffic congestion, parking, graffiti and dereliction (the Madeira Drive arches, for example) – just a few issues from a long list. Many areas are rundown (such as around St Bartholomew's Church) and, it could be argued, there is a somewhat 'tacky' feel to the city that other resorts like Eastbourne and Bexhill have somehow sidestepped.

The site for Churchill Square is cleared, 1965. Eighteen streets and courtyards were lost for this project.

In the past Brighton has been a health resort, military base, industrial town, holiday centre and conference facility, but what is it today? Time moves on and people spend holidays, weekends and days out differently from how they used to. Few things are manufactured in Brighton today and its population is more transient and far less concerned about what is lost or changed. It remains a resort for conferences, with the Brighton Centre a purpose-built, but now dated, facility. What it also has is two universities and an ever-increasing student population. The opening of Sussex University in 1962 was the beginning of a huge expansion of educational facilities in Brighton, which would include a new art college building in Grand Parade, a polytechnic in Lewes Road, a college of education for trainee teachers at Falmer and new facilities in the North Laine area for the technical college – all opening in the same decade. These buildings are now part of the 1992 Brighton University.

Educational expansion has led to an unprecedented demand for student accommodation, with the London and Lewes roads now teetering on becoming more campus sites than shopping and residential areas. Students may bring animation and diversity to the city, but few care about its past or the decisions made concerning its future. They are, generally, uncritical of their surroundings and capricious about local issues. Neither are they big spenders, so the economy of the city doesn't benefit much from their temporary presence. Brighton's future is uncertain.

The annual Brighton Festival and Pride celebrations remain extremely popular, and the crowds turn out for other events like the 'Paddle Round the Pier' fundraiser. The Theatre Royal, Dome and Brighton Centre continue to flourish, but a huge question mark has arisen over the future of the i360, where an eye-popping investment was made, but the return has been far less than what was forecast. Most parks and gardens seem neglected, attractions for families are few, the Marina is becoming a housing estate and even the Royal Pavilion, externally, looks a little shabby. Visitors to Brighton are not significantly increasing. Brighton has been down before, most notably just before and just after the First World War, but managed to totally resurrect itself to become one of Britain's foremost seaside resorts. However, this took brave decision making and considerable foresight to perceive how the town would expand and what its future needs would be. There was also the municipal pride and collective effort to ensure the vision was attainable. The provision of housing in the interwar years and during the 1950s was astounding. What is today's vision for Brighton from those who make the decisions?

Graffiti in Jew Street.

6

Lost Royal Associations

What made Brighton achieve its immense popularity, cause a massive increase in population and led to the building of many architectural gems was the presence of royalty in the town from 1783 until 1845. The Prince of Wales, later George IV, first visited in 1783. He took an immediate liking to the place, and, cutting a long story short, built the Royal Pavilion as his residence in the town. He died in 1830 after a ten-year reign, but visited Brighton far more than is generally supposed. He stayed for six months on two occasions – it's probably no coincidence that after the second of these half-yearly visits, Thomas Read Kemp decided to invest in the spectacular eastern 'town', which still bears his name.

George IV was followed by his brother, William IV, who was also fond of Brighton and visited regularly. William had no legitimate children, so his niece Victoria ascended to the throne in 1837. She didn't like Brighton, finding the people irksome and the Pavilion a drain on the royal purse. In 1850, she sold it to Brighton's commissioning body for £53,000, stripping it bare of all its furniture, fixtures and fittings (even the wallpaper came off), leaving a shell that has taken decades to restore to its former glory.

Above left: The Prince of Wales, later George IV. (Courtesy of the Metropolitan Museum of Art)

Above right: William IV. (Courtesy of the Wellcome Collection)

Princess Victoria, later queen. (Courtesy of the Yale Center for British Art, Paul Mellon Collection)

When these three monarchs were residing in Brighton, wealthy and titled visitors came too, leading to all manner of high-class housing, facilities and amenities being provided, including the town's first pier structure. Since those heady days, Brighton's royal visits have been occasional rather than frequent and no monarch stays for six months any more, as happened with George IV.

2

The Chain Pier

Brighton has had three piers over the course of its history. The Chain Pier was the first, opening in 1823 – more or less same time as the Royal Pavilion was completed. It wasn't a pleasure pier, it was an embarkation jetty for ships, so those visiting Brighton could travel on to Europe, to France and Belgium. It's seen here taking shape in 1822. For most of its length, it was only 13 feet wide.

The Chain Pier went out from the cliff below New Steine. The piles were wooden, with four cast-iron bridges, or pylons, along its length, which supported the chain-link arrangement that held it together. There's no record of George IV going on the pier, but both William IV and Queen Victoria made a number of visits. This view is from the 1880s.

Fireworks on the pier in 1856, celebrating the end of the Crimean War. The pier proved popular until the railway reached Newhaven in 1847, which had far better facilities for passengers, bringing about a sharp decline in traffic from Brighton. The West Pier, opening in 1866, impacted even further on its fortunes.

The pier was lost one night late in 1896, decimated by a tremendous storm; this view shows the scene the following morning. A landmark building had gone, but it was about to be demolished anyway. Work on its replacement had already started on a site further west, opposite Old Steine – the new Brighton Marine Palace and Pier (the Palace Pier). This would open in 1899.

3

The West Pier

Of all its amenities, the greatest loss to Brighton has been the West Pier. At present, its ruins stand in the sea, much photographed and referred to as 'iconic', but ultimately are a reproach to all involved in its demise and destruction. Here, around 1930, the pier is at the height of its popularity, with attractions including shows at its pier-head theatre, band concerts, paddle steamer trips, 'aquatic' performers and all manner of amusements and sideshows.

An early view of the pier, showing how at first it was just as an exceptionally elegant venue for promenading, taking in the sea air and listening to a band playing at the pier head. There were hardly any amusements on the pier to start with. As previously mentioned, the older Chain Pier, to the east, would now seriously decline in popularity.

Another early view, looking towards Regency Square, around 1870. At a half-yearly meeting of the directors early in 1875, it was reported that visitor numbers for the previous six months, not including season ticket holders, was 276,928. By 1880, the number of visitors had increased to 845,165 (presumably for the whole year).

This 1874 view shows a regatta taking place off the eastern side of the pier, with spectators benefiting from a low tide to get a closer view. As well as the serious racing there would be novelty competitions, such as an aquatic football match and walking the greasy pole (between girders of the pier), and the event would end with a tea party on a large raft.

New owners took over the pier in 1890 and, aware that plans were being finalised for the Palace Pier, decided to invest heavily in new amenities. These included a large pavilion on the pier head, which would later become a theatre. Extensive landing stages, for paddle steamer trips, were also planned.

Excursions on paddle steamers from both the West and Palace piers were extremely popular. On one occasion in 1898, nine vessels were queuing up alongside the pier. The picture here is much later and shows the *Waverely* about to leave for a trip in the mid-1930s. Excursions were along the south coast to places like Worthing, Hastings and Eastbourne. Day trips to the Isle of Wight also took place, as did visits to France.

Above and below: Entertainment on the West Pier: dodgem cars near the pier entrance in the 1930s, plus a daredevil stunt artist, the Great Omani, driving a speedboat blindfolded through the pier's substructure in 1960, with a petrol-covered sea set alight.

Above left, right and below: Neglect, lack of maintenance and massive indifference led to the pier head area being declared unsafe and closed off in 1970. Five years later, the whole structure was declared dangerous. Brighton's West Pier closed on a sunny afternoon on 30 September 1975. These views were taken that day.

There then followed an inordinately drawn-out effort to save the pier – too complex and tedious to relate here. The West Pier Trust was formed in 1978 to oversee restoration. £14 million of lottery money was secured, but would only be forthcoming if matched by the trust – money it didn't have. Developers came and went, as did dates for restoration and reopening, but nothing happened and parts of the pier collapsed, as here, in 1988.

Everyone knows how the saga of the West Pier ended. Brighton has been awash ever since with speculation about who was responsible for what was obviously an arson attack. Many say a boat approached the pier, several individuals boarded the structure, and the fire started after they left. None have been identified and the whole blaze remains mysterious and deeply concerning. This image is from 2003.

The ruins of Brighton's West Pier (1866–1975). The rest of the book shows other losses to Brighton, but the West Pier heads the list. It was completely unique and irreplaceable (the only Grade I listed pier to exist) and nothing like it will ever be seen again. Nationally, it was up there with Stonehenge, the Tower of London and Brunel's Clifton Suspension Bridge.

4

The Regent

For most Brightonians, the Regent Cinema, which stood in Queen's Road from 1921 until 1973, was Brighton's best picture house bar none. There was a dance hall on the roof, generally reckoned the finest outside London and a popular rendezvous for many courting couples. Both were designed by Robert Atkinson at a cost of £500,000 (around £12 million today). The ballroom was going to be in the basement but the excavations proved too costly, so it was added to the roof, opening in 1923.

The sumptuous original interior of the Regent Cinema, which showed silent films at first, accompanied by an orchestra. A fire occurred in 1929, leading not only to a rebuilt auditorium, but also, as the time was opportune, the installation of sound facilities, as the first 'talking pictures' were being released. The first to be shown was *The Singing Fool*, starring Al Jolson.

The Regent Dance Hall, probably not long after it opened, showing its 'jazzy' decor and band area on the right. Syd Dean, (inset) was leader of one of the most popular of the Regent's regular bands. Others to appear were led by Jack Hylton, Billy Cotton and Harry Roy.

Jiving taking place at the Regent in the late 1950s. Despite the Rank organisation (who owned it) spending £15,000 on new flooring in 1963, they closed the dance hall in 1967 and it became a bingo hall. In 1970, it was turned into the Big Apple, a venue for live concerts. Some of the biggest names in pop appeared here, including Donavan, T Rex, Pink Floyd, Ginger Baker, Status Quo, the Kinks and the Rolling Stones, but despite being well patronised, it closed the following year.

The cinema flourished until Rank opened a new three-screen Odeon in 1973 at the bottom of West Street, in their Top Rank centre, which was renamed the Kingswest. This resulted in the closure of the Regent and two other cinemas: the Academy and a 1930s Odeon, also owned by Rank, which were both located in West Street. The final film at the Regent was *Cabaret* in 1973; it had lasted fifty-two years. It's seen here derelict in 1974, a year before demolition. A large branch of Boots the chemists presently occupies the site.

5

The SS Brighton

Another extremely popular sporting and entertainment amenity was the SS Brighton, occupying a site near the bottom of West Street, on the western side. This was, for most of its life, an ice rink, where public skating sessions were held and spectacular ice shows were presented. The entrance is seen here in 1963.

Strangely, no photographs have come to light of the SS Brighton being built. It started as a swimming stadium in 1934, with a pool 165 feet long and 65 feet wide, the largest of its kind in the world. It was actually financed by the mayor of Bournemouth (and constructed by a Bournemouth firm), who had offered to build a pool there, but his plan was turned down so he made the proposal to Brighton. This view was taken the year it opened.

The pool didn't operate at a profit, as 1934 enjoyed a superb summer and trippers passed the building to swim in the sea free of charge. This photograph looks towards the shallow end and shows what an impressive amenity it was. New ice rinks that opened in the early 1930s at Wembley, Streatham and Southampton were proving popular, so the SS management converted the pool into a rink.

The rink was 175 feet by 75 feet and proved a success from the word go, attracting large numbers of skaters of all levels of ability. Further success followed when a new kind of entertainment on ice was offered on New Year's Eve in 1936, called *Viennese Memories*, remembered mainly for the absurdity of the costumes worn by the female dancers. However, the show was popular and a full-scale production, *Marina*, was arranged the following summer.

Above and left: A scene from *Marina* and one from the 1937 production that followed, *Patria*, billed as 'a Coronation Ice Cruise,' which celebrated George VI's coronation that year. Many different kinds of ice show were then held at the SS Brighton, including ice circuses, pantomimes and even musicals like *Rose Marie* and *The Wizard of Oz* adapted as ice spectaculars.

The stadium became a multipurpose building where a whole range of sporting events and meetings were held. Tennis, boxing, wrestling, basketball, judo, table tennis, plus political conferences and Rotary meetings (pictured here), were all accommodated, with the ice area covered with special flooring. Audiences sometimes complained of chilly feet as the coldness worked through and a standard joke during political conferences was that meetings were, 'all hot air and cold feet'.

Brother and sister John and Jennifer Nicks, both from Brighton, won a string of titles in pair's figure skating between 1947 and 1953. They were often seen rehearsing at the SS Brighton. Their father ran Wisden's sports shop in Duke Street. In 1953 the pair won the British, European and World Championship titles. In fact, they were British Champions six times in a row (1948–53) and came fourth in the 1952 Winter Olympics. They retired after their 1953 triumphs and John became a coach in South Africa, Canada and America; he was inducted into the World Figure Skating Hall of Fame in 2000. Jennifer died in 1980.

The ice show for the winter of 1950 was *Sleeping Beauty*. This ran for seventy-nine performances, sometimes three a day, opening on Christmas Eve and finishing in early February 1951. These shows would tell the traditional story, but intersperse all manner of specialities into the show, sometimes even animal acts, and there was always a spectacular scene or two involving special effects and transformations from one location to another. Seat prices for *Sleeping Beauty* ranged from 2s 6d to 10s 6d.

Above left: Of all the sports held at the stadium, ice hockey drew the biggest crowds and had the largest following. The town's home team, the Brighton Tigers, founded in 1935, were British champions three times – 1946–47, 1947–48 and 1957–58. In 1957 they even beat the Soviet national team, 6-3. The Tigers had a huge fan base, and it was said that during matches the cheering could be heard up at Brighton station. In this team photograph, left of the goalkeeper is manager Benny Lee; Alan Weeks, publicity manager, is on the right.

Above right: Bobby Lee (1911–74) was the Tigers' star player, the first in ice hockey to score 200 goals, when rivals at Streatham and Wembley had only managed 100 or so. He learnt the game on frozen rivers while growing up in Montreal, Canada, playing first at junior level for the local Montreal Royals, then the senior La Fontaine team. He joined the Tigers in 1934 and became player-manager, taking the team to giddy heights of success and popularity. Lee was inducted into the British Ice Hockey Hall of Fame in 1949 and retired five years later, becoming landlord of the Mile Oak Inn, then running the Windmill Inn at Southwick.

The year 1965 saw the final Tiger's match at the SS Brighton – the end of an era. The game was against the Paisley Mohawks, and the Tigers won (fortunately!). Following this, the SS was closed and demolished. The team could then only play away matches, and eventually were wound up. The Brighton Royals, formed in 1977, included some former Tiger players, but this folded in 1988.

Above: Why was such a well-patronised and much-loved building lost? The Rank organisation owned the SS and wanted the site as part of their Top Rank entertainment centre. This was going to be L-shaped with one part in King's Road and the other in West Street. This model (1964) shows Rank's intentions; it looks across West Street, with their entertainment centre left, which was fully built, and right – the SS site – to be developed as a restaurant and shopping area.

Right: Benny Lee watches the ice melt following the Tigers' final match. The SS came down in 1966. He said: 'The day the SS Brighton was demolished, they tore the sporting heart out of the town.' The last ice show was *Peter Pan* in 1963. To everyone's disgust, Rank decided not to build anything on the SS site, and it remained empty for almost a quarter of a century. Eventually, the Oak Hotel went up in 1991, later renamed the Quality Hotel.

6

Theatres

Above left: Brighton has had twelve full-sized, purpose-built theatres in its history, three of which survive – the Theatre Royal, the Hippodrome (at present derelict) and the Attenborough Arts Centre. There have also been a large number of smaller playhouses, of which Brighton Little Theatre and the Marlborough, among others, continue to flourish. Seen here was the fifth of the large theatres to be built, opening in 1863 as the Oxford Music Hall in New Road. This was run traditionally, with a chairman, twelve or so different acts and drinks served continuously throughout the performances. Three shops separated it from the Theatre Royal. It's pictured around 1910, when named the Court. This theatre had nine different names over the years, closing in 1962 when operating mostly as a cinema called the Paris.

Above right: An interior view of the Paris, just before demolition in 1963. The ports for showing films can be seen at the top. It looked very similar to the Theatre Royal at this time, even in its colour scheme, but lacked a gallery. Playwright J. B. Priestly said it was loveliest playhouse on the south coast. This would be the second longest-running theatre in Brighton's history.

Space precludes including all of the nine lost theatres, but this is the Alhambra, which opened in 1888, roughly where the eastern part of the Brighton Centre currently stands in King's Road. Music halls were being succeeded by variety shows at this time, and many top performers appeared here, including Marie Lloyd, George Robey and Florrie Ford, supported by a host of speciality acts. The main frontage was in Russell Street, off to the left; the entrance here, in King's Road, seen around 1905, was a converted shop. The theatre could seat 2,200 people.

The Alhambra became a cinema from 1912, known first as the Grand Cinema de Luxe, then the Palladium. Although it was converted into Odeon with a new art deco frontage in 1936 (seen here), its original interior theatre layout was retained, including the boxes. The name Odeon was changed back to Palladium when a new Odeon opened in West Street. It closed in 1956 and was demolished in 1963.

Both the Palace and West piers had theatres. This is the one on the Palace Pier, operating from 1901 until 1973, the third longest-running theatre in Brighton. World-famous ballet dancer Anna Pavlova appeared here in the 1920s. Productions were very much geared to the tastes of trippers visiting the pier and were usually lightweight comedies, musical revues and detective dramas, with pantomimes at Christmas.

The interior of the West Pier theatre, which opened in 1903. Some very famous performers appeared here, including Stan Laurel and Charlie Chaplin at the start of their careers. Rex Harrison, Edith Evans, Flora Robson and Ralph Richardson also appeared and plays were often more sophisticated than those on the Palace Pier.

Both the West and Palace piers closed during the Second World War. The Palace Pier theatre reopened, but the West Pier's was converted into a large amusement arcade. The closure of the Hippodrome in Middle Street, in 1964, saw summer variety revived on the Palace Pier, with Jack Tripp, Dick Emery and Ronnie Corbett starring in spectacular, big-budget shows.

The theatre was badly damaged in the autumn of 1973, when a 75-ton steel barge, in use dismantling the last of the landing stages at the pier head, broke free from its mooring in a storm and battered a number of piles until they gave way. A large part of the theatre dropped (seen here) and although it was repaired, it never reopened. The then new owners, the Noble Group, had it demolished in 1986.

The Grand was at the top of North Road, starting life as a circus named the Hippodrome, opening in 1891. This had no connection with the Hippodrome in Middle Street, which came later. It was claimed the building could seat 5,000 people, but had a short life due to the death of its owner. It was then converted into a theatre, the Eden, in 1894. In 1904, it became the Grand, a venue renowned for sensational melodrama, glittering pantomimes and adult glamour entertainment. This is *The Queen of Hearts* pantomime of 1928.

The Grand was converted into a cinema in 1931. However, during the Second World War many servicemen were billeted in Brighton and there was a demand for old-style shows. The Grand duly responded and managed to keep variety going again after the war, booking up-and-coming stars such as Tommy Cooper, Frankie Vaughan, Spike Milligan, Frankie Howerd and Petula Clark. Despite this, the Grand closed in 1955, ending its life in a spectacular fire in 1961, when in use as a furniture store.

The last purpose-built theatre in central Brighton was its largest – the Imperial, standing in North Street, at the corner of Windsor Street, opening in 1940. Initially, it held 1,877 people. It was renamed the Essoldo in 1950 (seen here) but, due to the onset of TV, struggled to find shows and acts, often becoming a cinema in between theatrical productions.

FIRST WEEK	
Monday, 25th March	*Bizet*
CARMEN	
GITA DENISE	NANCY CREIGHTON
PAULINE ALLEN	WILLIAM AITKEN
JOHN HEDDLE NASH	· FREDERICK WOOD
JOHN FAASSEN	DONALD CAMPBELL
Conductor : Arthur Hammond	

Tuesday, 26th March	*Verdi*
RIGOLETTO	
NANCY CREIGHTON	GLENICE HALLIDAY
WALTER MIDGLEY	JOSEPH SATARIANO
STANISLAV PIECZORA	ERNEST THOMAS
Conductor : John Bell	

Wednesday, 27th March	*Puccini*
MANON LESCAUT	
KRYSTYNA GRANOWSKA	CHARLES CRAIG
EDUARDO ASQUEZ	ARTHUR WALLINGTON
DONALD CAMPBELL	FREDERICK WOOD
Conductor : Arthur Hammond	

Thursday, 28th March	*Mascagni*
CAVALLERIA RUSTICANA	
RUTH PACKER GEORGE CHITTY JOSEPH WARD	
Conductor : Edward Renton	
followed by **I PAGLIACCI** *Leoncavallo*	
JOYCE GOODWIN	JOHN MYRDDIN
JOSEPH SATARIANO	JOHN FAASSEN
Conductor : John Bell	

Friday, 29th March	*Rossini*
THE BARBER OF SEVILLE	
GLENICE HALLIDAY	WILLIAM AITKEN
JOSEPH SATARIANO	JOHN HEDDLE NASH
STANISLAV PIECZORA	
Conductor : Anthony Addison	

Saturday, 30th March	*Gounod*
FAUST	
ESTELLE VALERY	JULIA BOUTTELL
PAULINE ALLEN	CHARLES CRAIG
JOHN HEDDLE NASH	STANISLAV PIECZORA
Conductor : Arthur Hammond	

SECOND WEEK	
Monday, 1st April	*Mozart*
DON GIOVANNI	
RUTH PACKER	KRYSTYNA GRANOWSKA
ESTELLE VALERY	EDUARDO ASQUEZ
JOHN HEDDLE NASH	STANISLAV PIECZORA
ERNEST THOMAS	
Conductor : Arthur Hammond	

Tuesday, 2nd April	*Puccini*
LA BOHEME	
ESTELLE VALERY	JOYCE GOODWIN
WILLIAM AITKEN	JOHN HEDDLE NASH
EVAN THOMAS	DONALD CAMPBELL
Conductor : Edward Renton	

Wednesday, 3rd April	*Wagner*
TANNHAUSER	
RUTH PACKER	GLENICE HALLIDAY
GEORGE CHITTY	EDUARDO ASQUEZ
ARTHUR WALLINGTON	STANISLAV PIECZORA
Conductor : Arthur Hammond	

Thursday, 4th April	*Verdi*
IL TROVATORE	
KRYSTYNA GRANOWSKA	JULIA BOUTTELL
WALTER MIDGLEY	JOHN FAASSEN
DONALD CAMPBELL	
Conductor : Arthur Hammond	

Friday, 5th April	*Berlioz*
BENVENUTO CELLINI	
ESTELLE VALERY	PAULINE ALLEN
CHARLES CRAIG	JOHN FAASSEN
STANISLAV PIECZORA	DONALD CAMPBELL
EDUARDO ASQUEZ	ERNEST THOMAS
Conductor : Arthur Hammond	

Saturday, 6th April	*Bizet*
CARMEN	
GITA DENISE	NANCY CREIGHTON
PAULINE ALLEN	GEORGE CHITTY
JOHN HEDDLE NASH	FREDERICK WOOD
JOHN FAASSEN	DONALD CAMPBELL
Conductor : Edward Renton	

Due to its enormous stage and large capacity, the Essoldo attracted many big touring operas, ballets and musicals. The programme here shows the astonishing repertoire of operas presented in a two-week visit by the Carl Rosa Opera Company in 1957. However, the popularity of even these high-calibre productions stalled and bingo took over from 1964 to 1995. In 1997 the building was revamped as the Hot Shots entertainment centre, but failed financially, leading to closure and demolition in 2001.

Brighton's most famous theatre was the Hippodrome in Middle Street, opening in 1902 and lasting until 1964. Every great variety and acting star would appear here over the years, including Marie Lloyd, Vesta Tilley (who haunts the building), magician Harry Houdini, Harry Lauder, Laurence Olivier, Vivien Leigh, Buster Keaton, Laurel and Hardy, Julie Andrews, Shirley Bassey, and Brighton's own comedian, Max Miller.

The Hippodrome actually started as an ice rink in 1897, but failed financially so was converted into a spectacular circus-theatre, seen here, by Frank Matcham, the leading theatre designer of the day. There were both stage and circus acts on the bill, but this mix didn't prove popular, so the building was again converted, this time to the variety theatre, which ran successfully for over sixty years.

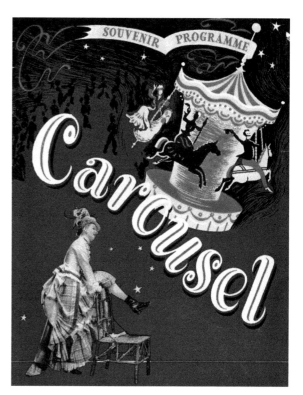

The Hippodrome always moved with changing tastes in entertainment. Variety was its mainstay over the years, with big bands popular in the 1920s and 1930s. Musicals like *The White Horse Inn*, *Oklahoma!*, *Carousel* and *Kiss Me Kate* attracted capacity crowds in the 1950s and early 1960s, but there were also plays, pantomimes and summer variety shows, plus ballet, opera and musical entertainment, such as appearances by the Red Army Choir.

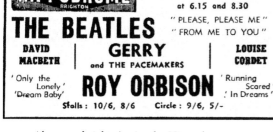

Above and right: Again, the Hippodrome was quick to respond to the trend in the late 1950s and early 1960s for pop concerts and booked some of the top performers of the day, including Tommy Steele, Cliff Richard, Gerry and the Pacemakers, the Rolling Stones and the Beatles, who appeared three times, the first as support for Roy Orbison. Obviously these would be sellouts, but in-between the Hippodrome still had to stage other shows.

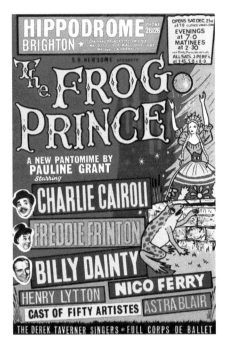

Time moves on, and by the early 1960s, mostly due to the impact of TV, the appeal of twice-nightly variety was fading, and the task of assembling a different weekly bill became increasingly difficult. Seen here is the flyer for the last pantomime, *The Frog Prince*, which ran from Christmas 1963 into early February the following year. An intriguing aspect of this show was when the princess lost a ball down a well and the frog (the prince under a spell) jumped in to retrieve it; a screen was lowered and his antics show as an animated film.

The Hippodrome closed in the autumn of 1964. The building served as a TV studio for a while, with plans coming and going to revive live entertainment again, one being for a 'Talk of the Town', cabaret-style venue. In the end, it succumbed to bingo in 1968, as seen here. This lasted until 2006. The building was then closed and its future decidedly uncertain; in early 2019 plans were announced for full restoration with the northern part of the building to become a hotel.

7

Cinemas

In 1960, Brighton possessed thirteen cinemas. These were the Academy, West Street; the Astoria, Gloucester Place; the Continental, Kemp Town; the Curzon, Western Road; the Duke of York's, Preston Circus; the Essoldo, North Street; the Gaiety, Lewes Road; the Odeon, West Street; a second Odeon, Kemp Town; the Paris, New Road; the Prices News Theatre, North Street; the Regent, Queens Road; and the Savoy, East Street. Several of these operated as theatres too. Pictured here is the Curzon, which started in 1909 as the Electric Bioscope, ending its days, after several name and façade changes, as the Classic in 1979. Of the thirteen cinemas listed, only the Duke of York's survives. There are two other multiscreen venues – one in West Street, the other at Brighton Marina.

The Academy opened in 1911 in a former Turkish bath building converted to create a 900-seat picture house. Films were silent then, but advertisements for the opening informed patrons there would be accompaniment by 'a full orchestra'. Its location, on the 'tripper track' from station to seafront, ensured its popularity and in 1913 it was enlarged to 2,000 seats. By then films had increased in length. *Quo Vadis?* was a huge hit in 1913 – one of the first full-length feature films to be made. A sound system was installed in 1929 and the Academy was completely rebuilt in 1938–39 (seen here), both inside and out. The work was done at night and early mornings, meaning the cinema could stay open, although patrons had to negotiate scaffolding when finding their seats. The cinema closed in 1973, with the last film being, ironically, *The Last Picture Show*.

In 2018 the Astoria Cinema was demolished. This, like the Regent and Savoy in East Street (detailed later), was a huge 'super cinema', opening in time for Christmas 1933 – it had been built in just five months. The auditorium (pictured here in 1958) could seat 1,823 patrons. It also had a stage, 42 feet across and 20 feet deep, dressing rooms and fly tower, meaning it could operate as a theatre, and a number of shows were staged, including pantomimes. The first film was *The Private Life of Henry VIII*.

Above left: *Earthquake* was the big attraction at the Astoria in 1975, which was presented in 'Sensurround', a system where the air in the cinema was vibrated, creating an impression the building was shaking. The Astoria's last film was the remake of *A Star is Born* in 1977. The building then served as a bingo hall, with several changes of ownership, becoming the Gala bingo club in 1972. 'Full house' was called in 1977 when Gala invested in new premises in Eastern Road. After years of wrangling over what should be done with the building, it was demolished for the inevitable rebuilding as flats.

Above right: The Savoy, so huge it backed onto Pool Valley, opened before the Astoria, in 1930. It's seen here in 1953. Another of the town's 'super cinemas', built at a cost of £20,000, it seated 2,630 patrons. In 1948, the world premiere of *Brighton Rock*, a film shot on location around Brighton, was held here.

The Savoy became an ABC Cinema in 1963 and in the early 1970s was a popular venue for live TV presentations of major sporting events. It was converted into a four-screen complex in 1976, which hastened the end of the single-screen Astoria. In 1986 it became part of the Cannon cinema chain (seen here in 1991), then an ABC cinema again, before closing in 1999. The building today is a casino and restaurant.

This Odeon, which opened in 1937 at a cost of £48,000, was the one that stood in West Street, adjoining the SS Brighton. It was originally to be called the Forum, but became part of the Odeon chain and the name was dropped. It could hold an audience of 1,920. It's pictured here when Anna Neagle and Anton Walbrook, stars of the 1937 film *Victoria the Great*, made personal appearances to promote the film.

James Bond is back! The Odeon is seen late in 1963, showing the Bond movie *From Russia with Love*. Despite £10,000 being spent on improvements in 1968, it closed in 1973 and the three-screen Odeon, mentioned on page 19, began operating two years later in the Rank entertainment complex further down West Street.

The very nondescript new Odeon, part of the 1973 Kingswest complex, is seen here with its odd escalator arrangement taking patrons to a second-floor entrance. This has now gone and the entrance is at ground-floor level. As well as the cinemas, the Kingswest housed Jenkinson's Cabaret Bar, the Revolution Disco, Papa Jenks Coffee Shop, plus a revamped Top Rank suite.

An Odeon was planned for Moulsecoomb in 1933, but failed to materialise. This one, in St George's Road, opened in 1934 at the corner of Paston Place, Kemp Town, and achieved lasting notoriety after receiving a direct hit from a German bomber in 1940. It lasted as a cinema until 1960, becoming a bingo hall two years later (seen here), then operated as a social centre, known as the City, from 1983. The building was demolished in 1986 and flats presently stand on the site.

The Gaiety (its first name), pictured here at the corner of Hollingdean Road, opened in 1937 with the musical *Swing Time*. It held an audience of 1,206 and was clearly built to serve north Brighton, including Elm Grove and Moulescoomb. It also entertained many troops stationed at Preston Barracks during the Second World War. The distinctive art deco-style frontage, over 50 feet high and neon lit at night, survived until 1965, when it was renamed the Ace and alterations were made.

The Ace was renamed the Vogue in 1970, then struggled to remain in business, becoming disreputable for showing adult glamour movies. It became the Classic in 1979, closing the following year. It was demolished for a new road system in the area, known as the Vogue gyratory, taken from the name the cinema once had. It's seen here derelict in 1983.

8

Other Amusements and Amenities

Brighton has provided so many attractions for visitors over the years, but space dictates only a few more can be included. Sherrys, at the bottom of West Street, was another extremely popular dance hall. The building started life as a large multipurpose hall in 1867, where concerts, meetings, dances and even roller-skating sessions were held. Sherrys opened here in 1919 as an 'Academy of Dancing' and soon became, along with the Regent, the leading dance venue in the town. Both were packed during the years of the Second World War, when large numbers of servicemen (particularly Canadians) were stationed in or around Brighton. Many marriages started on the floors of Sherrys and the Regent. Sherrys became immortalised in Graham Greene's 1938 novel *Brighton Rock*. Following the war, it saw mixed use, serving as a dance venue, bingo hall, skating rink and bar, retaining its name. The view here dates from 1960. When the Regent closed in 1967, the disco scene was really taking off, so Sherrys was rebuilt in 1969 to operate solely as a nightclub with a stage for bands. The name Sherrys was eventually dropped, and many clubs over succeeding years occupied the building – one was the Pink Coconut, which opened in 1983. Many changes of name and different managements have since come and gone, but the basic disco fare has remained the same.

Brighton used to have a waxworks, which can be seen under demolition in this view from 1981 following its closure two years earlier. This was Louis Tussaud's, in Grand Junction Road, virtually opposite the Palace Pier. The location is now part of the Royal Albion Hotel. It was small and very low key compared to present-day waxwork attractions and did little to promote itself. It opened in 1938, with musical star Jesse Matthews among its first celebrity figures.

This view of the Beatles figures at Tussaud's could be bought as a souvenir postcard in the 1960s. The likenesses were not considered particularly good. Other figures on show included a group from the TV soap *Coronation Street* (sat in the Rover's Return pub), sporting, TV and film personalities (such as Sean Connery), plus royalty and politicians. There was also a 'Chamber of Horrors' in the basement, featuring the Hunchback of Notre Dame swinging on a bell, a scene of Aztec sacrifice and a few well-known murderers. There was a Louis Tussaud's at Blackpool until 2010, but this was taken over by London's Madame Tussaud the following year.

Brighton also had a motor museum, which was in the Aquarium, located in a multi-purpose hall that had previously served as a ballroom, cinema and exhibition space. Speed legend Donald Campbell performed the opening ceremony in 1961. Over a hundred vintage cars, motorbikes and cycles were on display, including a 1935, 4.1-litre Daimler, once used by Queen Mary, and a 27-hp Humber, which was Field Marshal Montgomery's staff car.

The popularity of two dolphins introduced to the Aquarium in 1968 saw the end of the Motor Museum, with the area transformed into a large pool with spectator seating in 1969 so that full dolphin shows could take place. This became one of the town's top tourist attractions, with four shows a day. However, animal welfare groups pressurised the council into closing the pool in 1990. The two remaining dolphins, Missie and Silver (there had been four), were taken to the Caribbean for rehabilitation. The Aquarium was subsequently remodelled as a SeaLife centre, opening at Easter 1991.

The 1930s saw a spate of swimming pools built throughout Britain. Many were outdoor lidos and three were created in Brighton and its wider area – all close to the sea. These were at Black Rock, Rottingdean and Saltdean. Black Rock bathing pool stood off Madeira Drive, operating between 1936 and 1978. Here it is being built in 1936.

The pool was 165 feet in length and 60 feet wide, and the cost was £40,000. The opening ceremony was presided over by the mayor of Brighton, Edward Denne, but unfortunately there was a downpour so the speeches were made in the café. This view shows the Marine Gate flats under construction in the background, so dates from 1939.

A 'Miss Brighton' contest under adjudication at the poolside in 1967. The winner was twenty-year-old Carol Ann Bull of Denton Drive – number three in the line-up – later to marry Brighton councillor Geoffrey Theobald and eventually become mayor of Brighton. She won the grand sum of £20 in the contest. Miss Brighton events were organised by Brighton Council at this time and seen as good publicity for the town. In time, such contests fell out of public favour and so the council eventually dropped them, but they are sometimes promoted by various nightclubs in the town as part of the Miss Great Britain contest, which still takes place.

There was even once a zoo in Brighton, which was housed in Withdean Stadium, when it was mostly just tennis courts. Actress Jean Simmons performed the opening ceremony in 1948. It proved popular to start with, and was enlarged the following year. There were various 'houses' for lions, bears, monkeys and parrots, and a large-scale model railway gave visitors rides. However, it proved uneconomic to keep going and closed in 1952. The stadium was then converted into a centre for athletics, with a running track, which opened in 1955.

Left and below: Three views of Peter Pan's Playground in Madeira Drive. This opened after the Second World War on a site previously occupied by bowling greens. It expanded in the 1950s, offering more rides and attractions. Seen here are the 'Jungle Express', roller-skating rink, plus a general view of other amusements. The playground was still operating in the early 1990s, but eventually closed, with plans for an open-air swimming pool and other new facilities on the site yet to materialise.

A novel attraction at Peter Pan's from the 1930s through to the late 1960s were these 'midget' buses that children could ride in – perfect replicas of those operated by the well-known firm Southdown. They were built by local man Ernest Johnson in a building known as the Old Forge in Preston village. He made nearly seventy vehicles in all – mostly buses, but also a few fire engines. A few have survived and two are displayed at the motor museum at Rolvenden, Kent.

A very recent seafront attraction was the £6 million Brighton Wheel, which opened in 2011. It was 45 metres in diameter and could carry 284 visitors in its thirty-five capsules. Built in Germany, the structure was 'fully transportable', first used in Paris, then Cape Town in 2010, serving fans attending the FIFA World Cup. The wheel came to Brighton when plans for the proposed i360 viewing tower initially floundered. The council allowed it to operate with a limited licence until 2016. When the i360 was completed, it had to be dismantled.

9

Streets and Housing

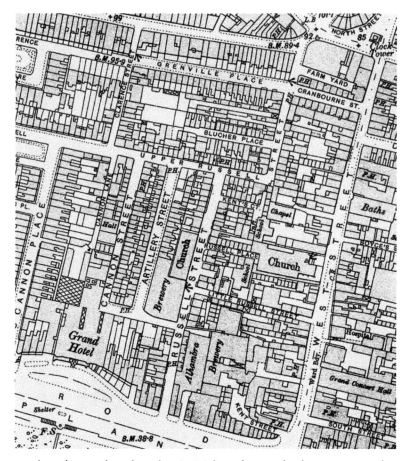

A huge number of streets have been lost in Brighton for one development or another, mostly consisting of housing, which is now particularly ironic, with the dire shortage of accommodation being a paramount issue in the city today.

This map of 1909 shows what stood on the site of the present-day Churchill Square area. Today the shopping mall occupies the area towards the top, car parks the central area and the Brighton Centre and the Pryzm entertainment building (originally the Top Rank centre) the bottom. The top road, unnamed, is Western Road. West Street is on the right, King's Road is at the bottom and Cannon Place is to the left. These border a network of streets, a brewery, meat factory, school, pubs, shops, several chapels and the Alhambra theatre (previously mentioned) – a complete, almost self-contained, community.

On this and succeeding pages are photographs of some of the streets and buildings seen on the map that were demolished for the scheme. Grenville Place ran parallel to Western Road on its southern side. The first reference to this street comes in a storm report in a *Brighton Herald* of 1806, when it was stated that four houses in the street 'in an unfinished state' were virtually blown down. The southern side, seen here in 1963, was particularly attractive. The street was fully cleared in 1967.

This was probably the finest property in the area. Milton House, with its pebble-dash rendering, is seen standing in its own grounds right at the end of Milton Place. Its frontage was in Clarence Street. Very little is known about this property, but it was once smaller (the left part is an extension) and was probably built around 1820. The view here shows it in the early 1900s. All the smaller dwellings of Milton Place had been demolished by 1962, and the house was last to go, at the end of 1964.

Russell Street and Upper Russell Street, named after Dr Richard Russell, one of the physicians who vigorously advocated the seawater cure back in the mid-1700s, were semi-derelict at the time of the Churchill Square development. This early 1920s view is of Russell Street, which ran northwards from King's Road, between West Street and the Grand Hotel. It was first built up by a developer named Stephen Paine from 1788. Note the pub in the distance, the Good Intent. A disused church is in use as a meat factory on the left.

As the map shows, Upper Russell Street ran west to east, across the top of Russell Street, then turned north at a right angle, coming out at Western Road. A tiny part still exists today near the steps leading up to Churchill Square from Cranbourne Street. This 1930s view was taken in that area, and looks south from Western Road, down Upper Russell Street, towards where it turns westwards (right). The Cranbourne Arms pub can be seen; the building is named the Western today.

Artillery Street can be found virtually in the centre of the map. This had housing on its western side, with part of a brewery, the Cannon, on the other, with a couple of houses right at the top. A pub, the Artillery Arms, stood at the corner with Western Road. The houses were still occupied during the mid-1950s, but were compulsorily purchased on health grounds, then demolished.

The Cannon Brewery, Nos 10–16 Russell Street, is seen from the air in the early 1960s. Artillery Street stands with nothing on its western side. Russell Street is on the extreme right. The brewery started in the smallest of ways, in a house in Russell Street that was owned by John Barnett, who sold home-brewed beer from a cart. He founded the Cannon Brewery, which successive owners built up into a thriving business, owing some fifty pubs. Brewing stopped in 1929 and the building was used for storage and bottling. It closed after a compulsory purchase order was made in 1965.

The meat factory, seen on the western side of Russell Street, was actually a converted church, the Church of the Holy Resurrection, built mostly below ground level in 1876–77 to serve the area. This is the interior in the early 1900s. It closed in 1909 and was subsequently used, from 1912, as a cold meat store, housing a number of businesses and becoming Brighton's central meat market. The Cannon Brewery stood just below it. Both were demolished in 1968.

Many streets of housing were lost for what was called the Albion Hill Redevelopment Scheme, starting in the late 1950s and largely completed by 1966. This early 1920s view, from the tower of St Peter's Church, shows most of the area 'as built', running south from Albion Hill to Edward Street, a warren of congested streets, much of it slum property. At the 1921 census, Brighton was one of the most densely populated towns in the whole of Britain, second only to West Ham.

A look up Richmond Street in the early 1900s, with the tower of Richmond Street School visible on the right-hand side of the street. This was a district of Brighton that was populous enough to be virtually self-sufficient in its needs, with many varied shops, pubs, several schools and small workshops and servicing premises, plus, surprisingly, a farm.

Here is the farm, originally of 30 acres, nestled within the packed housing of the area. It operated from around 1862 until 1934 and was known as the Richmond Farm Dairy and owned by William Chate. The farm buildings are in the centre, to the right. The site today is partly occupied by the Chates Farm Court flats in John Street, which opened in 1980, preserving the old name.

The only surviving farm building (seen on the right of this 1910 view) is a wing of the farmhouse at the angle of what remains of Richmond Street as it turns now into Elmore Road – No. 34a. Some of the other buildings survived as garages until 1977. As well as cows, there were horses, ducks, chickens, rabbits and homing pigeons, with land ploughed for fodder and growing vegetables.

The Albion Hill redevelopment saw much of the area cleared (some rebuilding had taken place in the 1930s) and Brighton's first six high-rise blocks of flats built, with nobody really aware of their impact on both the street profile and the lifestyle of their residents. This view, taken from Theobald House (just built in the Cheapside area), dates from 1966. Compare this with the earlier 1920s picture. The trend for such buildings was then up and running in Brighton and has continued, unrelentingly, ever since.

Nearby Edward Street (to the south) has changed out of all recognition, and was originally half the width it is today. It's seen here in the early 1900s. It was widened over many years, starting in 1927 at the Grand Parade corner, when the terrace of housing on the left was demolished to allow traffic easier access into Edward Street. Other properties on the northern side would be cleared in the 1930s up to Riding School Lane. Then, after the war, work resumed in the Mighell Street area and beyond.

The northern side of Edward Street, opposite Dorset Gardens, in 1938, prior to demolition. The intervening street is George Street Gardens. Edward Street was, in the past, very similar to St James's Street, as it was lined with shops on both sides, with all the usual bakers, grocers, greengrocers and butchers, but some were unusual or specialist. For example, in 1954, at No. 163 (just above Dorset Street) there was a firm named Masks and Mouldings Ltd, a 'manufacturers of carnival, children's and dolls' masks'.

Looking down Edward Street to Grand Parade in 1961. The Great Globe pub is in the centre. By now, the widening plan had grown into creating a full dual carriageway to Arundel Road, Kemp Town. Park Street was reached by 1970, but although other clearance had taken place on the southern side of Eastern Road (see p. 61), the plan was abandoned, leaving the huge bottleneck by the Royal Sussex County Hospital, which all using the area, either on foot or in vehicles, still have to contend with.

Mighell Street, running north from Edward Street, is seen here with its pub, the Black Lion, halfway along it. This view was taken late in 1972, prior to the street being cleared for the first American Express building, which opened in 1977, completely changing the topography of a huge area on the northern side of Edward Street. However, a small section of Mighell Street survives, at the Carlton Hill end, containing an old listed farmhouse of the early 1800s.

Here is the American Express building, which was demolished in 2018 for a development known as the Edward Street Quarter. It came down when new premises for the firm were built in Carlton Hill, making the Edward Street building available for redevelopment. This would become, according to the council's brief, 'An open, vibrant, mixed-use quarter based on a flexible "campus-style" format which maximises its employment potential and acts as a model for urban design and sustainability.' Quite what that means remains to be seen.

The Cheapside area is another that has changed out of all recognition, starting in the early 1950s. This was, again, mostly due to a large number of substandard houses in the district. Pictured here are properties in Blackman Street, which were compulsorily bought by the council in 1959 and demolished three years later. The nineteen-storey Theobald House partly occupies the site.

The site of the Cheapside redevelopment went right though to New England Road. This is New England Street, looking north from the York Hill end, which again was bought up by the council and demolished in 1958. New England House, opening in 1963, was built on the eastern side, housing small units of light industry. The street was subsequently extended southwards towards St Bartholomew's Church.

In the 1980s, King Street, running from North Street to Church Street, was decimated by a multistorey car park that was built right across it, dividing the street in two. This view looks south from Church Street in 1963, showing its attractive scale and individuality. Today, standing on the same spot, a few of the shops to the right survive, but the wall of a car park now straddles the street, blocking the other end completely out.

Another example of thoughtless planning was the removal of this terrace of housing in Waterloo Place, opposite the lower end of the Level. It was built just a few years after the famous battle of 1815 and was designed by Amon Wilds, whose partnership with Charles Busby produced many outstanding houses, terraces and crescents in Brighton. The properties here came down between 1968 and 1974 (one resident, aged eighty-nine, would not sell up, delaying the rebuilding) and Wellesley House was built on the site, which was later renamed Phoenix Brighton after the Phoenix Brewery, once located just north of the site.

10

Churches

Above and left: Victorian church life in Brighton was dominated for fifty years by Henry Mitchell Wagner (above left), vicar of Brighton during 1824–70, and his son Arthur Douglas Wagner (above right), who had the odd title of 'Perpetual Curate' of St Paul's Church, West Street. Was he forever learning his role? Between them, they financed eleven churches in the town, six of which have been lost. All Souls was their first, which stood in Eastern Road from 1833 until 1968. It was built to serve what was then a very poor area of Brighton, with many streets of cheaply built housing, such as Essex Street, Warwick Street and Bedford Buildings, all later to be demolished as slums. This view dates from the early 1900s. The church tower had four bells and there was an extensive crypt containing many tombs, the earliest dating from 1837.

The interior of All Souls Church, probably in the 1950s. The church was enlarged and altered several times during its 135 years of life. Six of the stained-glass windows were by Charles Eamer Kempe (he added the 'e' to his surname so he wouldn't be confused with Thomas Read Kemp, founder of Kemp Town). These survived the demolition of the church and were 'archived' in the Glazier's Hall repository, Montague Close, London. Another one went to Norwich Cathedral.

All Souls was demolished for the abortive road-widening scheme, mentioned earlier, where the proposed dual carriageway created in Edward Street would continue through to Kemp Town. This view of 1967 looks eastwards along Eastern Road, approaching All Souls. Clearance work has started. Upon demolition, the tombs in the crypt would be removed and reburied in the Bear Road Cemetery.

Another lost Wagner church was St Anne's in Burlington Street – their eighth. Built in 1862, it closed in 1983 after the parish amalgamated with neighbouring St George's. This view was taken a year later. Demolition followed in 1986 for the building of flats – St Anne's Court. The church institute building, of 1912, still stands in St George's Road.

The last church the Wagner's built, the Church of the Holy Resurrection, was detailed on page 52. The surviving Wagner churches are St Paul's in West Street, St Bartholomew's off London Road, St Martin's in Lewes Road, the Church of the Annunciation in Washington Street and St John's, Carlton Hill. The interior of St John's is seen here around 1970. It was made redundant in 1980, but from 1985 became a Greek Orthodox church. The interior was gutted by fire in 2010 and much altered when restored.

Other demolished churches in Brighton, not built by the Wagners, include the spectacular Dials Congregational Church, seen here a few years before demolition in 1979. It stood at the junction of Clifton and Dyke roads from 1870, its huge tower being a landmark of the area. An institute building directly adjoining the church had been built in 1881.

A close-up view of the Dials Congregational Church façade. The style is always given as Romanesque and resembled German churches seen when travelling down the Rhine. It was an astonishing building, particularly as the architect, Thomas Simpson, mostly designed thoroughly practical municipal buildings (many Brighton schools were to his plans) far removed from the flamboyance seen here. This made its loss all the more regrettable. It was replaced by a nursing home.

St Matthew's Church stood on the corner of Sutherland Road and College Terrace, and was built in 1881–83. Its tower was never completed, probably due to finance. Drawings show it was going to be three times the height of the building. The church replaced a much smaller, more basic building of 1879. It was demolished in 1967, with the parishioners joining St Mark's in Eastern Road. Flats occupy the site today – St Matthew's Court.

A really elegant church built in 1824, St Margaret's, stood at the western end of what would become St Margaret's Place. It was a speculative venture by Richard Gregory, named after his wife, to serve the wealthy areas of Regency Square, Russell Square and Cannon Place, all being built at the time. There was a charge for attending (rented pews) and Gregory hoped to make money on his undertaking. Clearly he didn't, however, as he sold the church off in 1827.

St Margaret's was restored in the 1870s, when the chancel was added. It lasted until 1956, closing, as with so many others, due to dwindling attendance. Plans to convert it into a costume museum fell through, despite an outstanding collection being offered – which went to Bath. Antony Dale, founder of the Regency Society, considered this the finest classical church Brighton ever had. It was demolished in 1959. The lower floors of the Sussex Heights flats now occupy the site.

A church that was strangely hidden from view, St James's, was at the corner of St James's Street and Chapel Street. Originally a chapel of 1813 (so naming Chapel Street), it was considerably enlarged in 1875. It contained nineteen stained-glass windows. This view, of around 1910, shows the St James's Street entrance, which was about all that could be seen as the bulk of the building was concealed by shops. A dwindling congregation saw St James's closed in 1948, with demolition following three years later.

Another hidden church was the Strict Baptist Chapel, off West Street, partly on the site of the present Wagner Hall in Regency Road. This was usually referred to as the Tabernacle, dated from 1834 and was originally used by evangelists. It became a Baptist chapel in 1842. It's seen here when the frontage was revealed during the widening of West Street in the 1930s, although it was soon to be concealed again when properties were rebuilt.

An early 1900s view inside the Baptist chapel, with its peculiar, lyre-shaped pulpit, plus the access to it from a door halfway up the wall. The last service was late in 1965 and the church moved to a new building in Montpelier Place (recently came down). The old chapel was demolished in 1965 as the site was needed for an access road from West Street to the car park area of the Churchill Square complex.

11

Public Baths

In the past, as everywhere, many Brighton homes lacked bathrooms. To fully wash, it was a case of filling a tin bath with water boiled on the kitchen stove or visiting a public bath building, of which there were four in Brighton. This flyer, dated 1932, details three of these buildings, the cost of bathing and the hours they were open.

One set of Corporation baths were off North Road in Barrack Yard. Opened in 1871, these were well patronised by families from the many terraced streets of the North Laine area. An *Evening Argus* of April 1976 reported:

> Last week marked the end of a Brighton era; the old North Road slipper baths finally closed its doors. The baths will be remembered by those who lived through the days when having a bathroom made you 'posh.' Declining attendances have forced Brighton council to close the baths, but even so more than 250 people took a soak in them during March. That may sound a lot, but compared with an average monthly attendance of more than 1000 people last year and more than 2500 in 1960, it represents a substantial drop in the bathwater.

A photograph of the public baths in Park Street, which were built in 1887 in celebration of the Golden Jubilee of Queen Victoria. The clock tower at the top of North Street was also built to commemorate the event. These baths opened in 1888 to serve what was the 'backstreet' area of Brighton, southwards off Eastern Road, mentioned on p.61.

There was absolute segregation of the sexes in all these bath buildings – in the waiting areas and even the entrances. This view is inside the Park Street building, showing a corridor with bath cubicles on either side. Circular taps can be seen, which would be turned by an attendant to fill the baths; a precise amount of water was allocated and bathing time limited.

One of the actual baths of the Park Street building is seen here, looking very spartan and old-fashioned, in 1977. As modern housing provided people with their own bathrooms, or existing houses were modernised, the need for bath buildings lessened. Park Street Baths closed in 1980, despite still being well patronised. In 1978, 15,000 baths were taken.

Another public bath building stood at the end of Cobden Road, at the corner of Islingword Road, opening in 1894. This served the Hanover area, surviving until 1976. The building then became the Hanover Community Centre until 1982. This view dates from 1984, when it was up for sale. There were three first-class baths for men, two for women, six second-class baths for men and four for women. The conversion into flats took place in 1985–86, with the entrance displaying the commemorative stone unveiled by Sir Joseph Ewart, mayor of Brighton, when the baths were inaugurated.

There was another public bath building not listed on the 1932 flyer, as it had closed the previous year. This originally stood at No. 46 Brunswick Place North, at the corner of Rose Hill Terrace, operating from 1891. Brunswick Place North became part of Ditchling Road shortly afterwards, with the baths renumbered No. 93, standing between Rose Hill Terrace and Viaduct Road. The photograph here of this building – now flats – was taken very recently. The two doors survive, once the separate entrances for men and women.

12

Shops

Where to start with all the well-known shops that have disappeared from Brighton's streets? Hanningtons, its most famous department store, once stood on an L-shaped site at the northern end of East Street, continuing round into North Street. It began trading in 1808 from a single shop at No. 3 North Street, with adjoining property acquired as the firm expanded. Hanningtons became well known for its many promotional events to attract customers, such as fashion shows, beauty evenings and competitions. It managed to keep going until 2001, but, along with other similar stores, couldn't compete with designer discount chains and out-of-town shopping malls.

Not far from Hanningtons, further up North Street, was Vokins, another department store, which began as a single shop in 1882 and was run by W. H. Vokins and his partner W. T. Leeson (the firm was then known as Leeson and Vokins). The business prospered and expanded, but the partnership came to an end in 1925. Vokins closed its Brighton store in 1997, not long after its centenary, but continues to trade as Big Brand Beds at Burgess Hill.

Leesons had this huge store for many years in North Street, just above the Clock Tower. It was originally built for Sopers, a drapers, another well-known Brighton firm (S. Soper was mayor of Brighton in 1890), which traded here until 1940. It was acquired by Leesons after the war, operating until 1954, when this picture was taken. The premises then split into three smaller units.

Everyone remembers F. W. Woolworth. This is their store in St James's Street, at the corner of Dorset Gardens, which opened in 1927. Modernised and extended in the 1960s, it closed in 1986. The first Woolworths in the UK opened in 1909 in Liverpool, part of a US company that started trading in 1879. The firm was hugely popular in its day, selling a vast variety of merchandise, including their own brands. The last of Woolworths's 807 British outlets closed in 2009 and the firm went into liquidation, with huge debts caused by falling trade.

The Brighton Equitable Co-Operative Society had its first shop in Brighton as far back as 1888, in North Road. This is their massive London Road emporium, which opened in 1931 and was designed by the partnership Bethel and Swannell. The frontage was 180 feet across, with four floors housing the various departments. The premises were enlarged in 1962, 1975 and 1980, the floor space rising to 70,000 square feet. As with other big stores featured in this section, it eventually operated at a loss, closing in 2007, with the building demolished (the frontage was kept) and mostly student accommodation built on the site.

Shops on the southern side of Western Road prior to demolition in 1967 for the Churchill Square redevelopment – the last properties to go for the project. Many well-known firms traded here, including Home and Colonial, the Scottish Wool Shop, Ernest Ward (fruiterers), Mac Fisheries, Dewhurst (a butchers) and Barratts.

Johnson Bros' home furnishing department store, also in Western Road, was founded by H. Betram Johnson (when he was just eighteen years old) and James, his brother, in 1902. The firm prospered and extensive workshops were established in Marlborough Street, where cabinetmaking, French polishing, carpet sewing and curtain making were undertaken. Fire wrecked the store in 1970, and although it was rebuilt (seen here in 1975), it was a smaller building and less profitable. The firm continued trading until 1979.

Forfar's, a popular local bakers, would have celebrated its bicentenary in 2018 had it not suddenly stopped trading in 2015. Shops in Brighton (their St James's Street store is seen here), Hove, Hassocks and Rustington were closed, along with the firm's bakery in Newhaven. The closures were all the more startling as Forfar's had registered a net worth of more than £1.3 million in October 2011, but the figure had dropped to a loss of over £670,000 at the end of 2013.

J. Lyons's 1927 premises at the corner of St James's Street, seen in the 1960s. There were four Lyons café-restaurants in Brighton, all well patronised in their day, partly due to their famous waitresses. Another was in Western Road and two were in North Street. They all closed in the 1970s, when the firm was sold off due to trading losses. Lyons had been established in 1885 and the brand name continues on cakes and biscuits as part of the Premier Foods range.

13

Schools

Again, the lost schools of Brighton can only receive token coverage. This one has to start this section as its loss was particularly unfortunate. Known as the National Schools, it stood in Church Street from 1829, opposite the end of New Road, and was built in Regency Gothic style. It lasted right through to 1967 (then known as the Central Schools) and was demolished four years later for proposed road widening. Antony Dale said: 'Despite the known intention to place the building on the Department of Environment's list of buildings of architectural interest it was demolished during the postal strike of 1971when communication was impossible. The gaping void is an obscene reminded of the criminal folly of this demolition.' The road widening wouldn't come until the Jubilee Street redevelopment, which started in 2003.

The Brighton Secondary Technical School, in Hanover Terrace, has to be included, as one of its pupils was the author of this book. An all-boys' school, it's seen here around 1970, when the timetable included metalwork or woodwork lessons twice a week. It started in 1873 as the Hanover Board School. It then took infants, mixed juniors and mixed seniors, but from 1928 it took just the junior and senior boys. The school nearly closed due to falling numbers in the 1940s, but carried on with just senior boys, becoming the Brighton Secondary Technical School. As so much practical work was undertaken, many local firms, including Allen West and the GPO, offered apprenticeships to those leaving the school. The BSTS ended its days as an annexe to Patcham Fawcett School, closing in 1981. It then became a centre for the disabled. In 1999, planning permission was granted for housing on the site, with demolition following in 2000.

Queen's Park Infants School, in Freshfield Place, was the author's first school. This opened in 1889, replacing an older institution in Eastern Road of 1826. A senior school was on the same site, facing Park Street. This photograph was taken in 1986, following closure at the end of the summer term. It was rapidly demolished, with the site becoming part of the old secondary school playground. This building still exists, but is now Queen's Park Primary School.

Nearby St Mary's School, in Mount Street, opened in 1873, replacing an earlier ragged school. It was initially named the Julius Elliot Memorial Schools, after the son of one of the vicars of St Mary's Church, who was killed while mountain climbing in Switzerland. The salary of the first head teacher was £3 a month. It became St Mary's Middle School in 1973, with 135 pupils. The school was bought as part of a housing redevelopment scheme for the area, with demolition coming in 1978.

This school in Circus Street was demolished in 2018, when the whole of the eastern side was redeveloped as high-rise flats, student apartments and a dance studio. It was built in 1884 to serve the densely populated Edward Street, Carlton Hill and Sussex Street area. It closed in 1935, when redevelopment of the area was imminent (the Circus Street market was built); however, it wasn't demolished, becoming an annexe for several nearby buildings, including the Clinic in Sussex Street.

St Paul's School, pictured here in 1961, stood behind the church in West Street and can be found on the 1909 map (page 48). This opened in 1877. As clearance for Churchill Square and its adjoining car parks progressed, the church authorities received £44,000 for the school, which was used to build brand new premises in Centurion Road, which opened in 1968. The crucifix from All Souls Church, Eastern Road, was installed in the hall. The old school was demolished in 1967.

The Xaverian College, a boys' Catholic school, occupied this 1830 villa north of Queen's Park, opening in 1909 on a part-boarding, part-day basis. Famous pupils included actor Ralph Richardson and Chelsea footballer Peter Bonetti. The college was sold to the De La Salle Order in 1961, moving to the Upper Drive in Hove five years later. Once vacated the villa became derelict and badly vandalised, leading to demolition in 1972 despite its Grade II* listing.

This is Brighton's original art college building, which opened as the New School of Science and Art in Grand Parade in 1877 by Princess Louise and her consort, the Marquess of Lorne. This was used until the early 1960s, when it was demolished and replaced – in three stages – by the present, more extensive building, which opened in 1967. The terracotta panels on either side of the entrance were retained and are presently displayed on the ground-floor walls.

14

Industry

Above and below: In 1960, Brighton's fish market, on the lower promenade, was closed by the council. This was after centuries of fishermen trading from the beach, then in a purpose-built market building and adjoining hard of the 1860s. Fishing was, with agriculture, the main industry of Brighton in the past, an institution that would seemingly never change. Many fishermen could trace their ancestry back several generations. Fish were regularly sold by auction from the hard, attracting large crowds of onlookers, and were a source of fresh fish for many hotels and boarding houses. Fishing mostly took place off the north-east coast of Britain, but some was done locally, if conditions were right. The comings and goings of the fishermen's boats, plus all the activity associated with trading, gave vitality and colour to the central beaches – now completely gone. The beaches really sprang to life when it was 'all hands to the capstan' to wind a boat up the beach.

The seafront fish market was closed by the council in 1960 (this view is of 1957, when the plan was first proposed). A new building was provided in Circus Street (described by one fisherman as 'a glorified portacabin'), but the lack of consultation and dismissive way the closure was handled caused deep resentment, which is still lingering today among some of the old fishing families of Brighton.

Another loss to the beach scene has been the Skylark pleasure yachts, with the cry 'Any more for the Skylark?' originating in Brighton. These boats were always associated with Captain Collins, one of the great characters from Brighton's past, who started boat trips in 1852. Skylarks were huge yachts at this time, taking up to eighty people for trips out to sea. The one here, a much smaller vessel, is pictured working in the 1950s. The last Skylark trips were in 1976, although there was a brief revival in 2000.

The biggest brewery in Sussex was once in Brighton. The Phoenix Brewery, in Richmond Terrace, seen here in 1970, was named when Richard Tamplin's Southwick brewery burnt down in 1820 and he opened new premises in Brighton, which 'rose from the ashes'. By 1902, there were 150 employees. The firm would eventually own 600 public houses, many in Brighton and Sussex but others in Kent, Hampshire and Surrey. The business was bought by Watneys in 1953, along with 400 of the pubs. Brewing ceased in 1973, with the main buildings coming down in 1980. Some were kept for bottling and storage until finally vacated in 1991, with operations moving to Lewes. The site is now mostly housing.

The main rival to the Phoenix, the Kemp Town Brewery was started in the 1830s as the Bristol Brewery by William Hallett (another Brighton mayor) in Seymour Street. This became the partnership Hallett and Abbey in 1854, and from around 1890 was known as Abbey & Sons. The name Kemp Town Brewery was taken in 1908 and the firm grew by the acquisition of a number of other brewing businesses. The company was taken over by Charringtons in 1954. Brewing stopped in Brighton ten years later, with the firm continuing production from new premises at Newhaven. The old brewery came down in 1970, along with a large malthouse at the bottom of Sutherland Road.

In the past Brighton was a town that made and built many things, with scores of factories and industrial premises employing thousands of local people in various manufacturing trades. A top employer in its day was the railway works, adjoining the main terminus building in Queen's Road, where railway engines were built. This aerial view, taken in 1920, which it's hard to believe is actually Brighton, shows the astonishing size of the works – all 9 acres of it.

In 1891, the works employed 2,651 people, many living in the surrounding streets of North Laine. This photograph shows the locomotive *Fernhurst* under construction in 1904. The premises had its own foundry where various ores arrived to be smelted to obtain the metal. This was then made into sheets or cast in moulds to make all the components to build the engines. At the height of its productivity, a fully operational railway engine could be made from scratch in four weeks.

During the Second World War, engines were being built at Brighton in less than a week. Railway nationalisation came in 1948, and although the works were in decline by then, there were still 650 staff in 1952 and the site remained the same size. The last engine made at Brighton (seen here) was in 1957. The works closed in 1962, with production transferred to other depots and most of the premises came down in 1969. A car park occupied the site until the building of the New England Quarter housing estate from 2004 to 2008.

Allen West, a firm that made an extensive range of electrical equipment, operated from the Lewes Road area and was another key employer in Brighton. It started in 1910 and grew to become one of the UK's largest manufacturers of control mechanisms and switchgear in the twentieth century. The company once employed over 3,000 people, with branches and representatives across the world. Their first premises are seen here on the right in the 1960s (demolished in 1972), plus a 1930s extension above it.

The firm expanded to Moulsecoomb Way in 1939, with several new factories built in the 1950s. The picture shows how massive just one of these was – 120,000 square feet of production space. Their 1930s premises became Mithras House, then part of Brighton Polytechnic. The slow decline of the firm started in the 1960s, resulting in all the Moulescoomb works eventually closing. It's hard to believe the firm ended up in premises in Hughes Road with a staff of just ten. It was wound up in 2018.

Cox's, a pharmaceutical business, was founded by Arthur Cox at No. 32 Ship Street in 1839. He was mayor of Brighton in 1882–83. Cox patented both the pearl-coated pill (to ease swallowing) and the sugar-coated pill (to improve taste). The firm expanded to take in No. 10a St Martin's Place in 1884. The move to Lewes Road, into former laundry premises, came in 1910–11. The factory is seen here, probably at the time of the Second World War, judging by the white kerb markings, which was used to aid vehicles driving in the blackouts.

A view inside Cox's factory in the early 1970s. After years of trading successfully, the premises became outdated and unable to maintain the hygiene regulations required for a drug company. The firm moved to the Whiddon Valley, Barnstable, in 1976 and the building came down in 1983, to be replaced by a huge Sainsbury's superstore, which is still operating today.

There were once many blacksmiths and forges in Brighton. This was one of the last to survive, which was run by Arthur Dawkins at No. 1 Marshall's Row, near the entrance to the Open Market, off London Road. Many Brightonians vividly recall seeing a horse reshod here, with all the accompanying sights and smells. The Dawkins family owned this forge for over seventy years. Arthur died in 1967 and the premises were sold off for £16,150.

15

Transport

It was once possible to catch a train from Brighton station and travel to Kemp Town station, where, at present, the Gala Bingo hall stands, near Brighton College. This was the Kemp Town Railway, constructed by the London, Brighton & South Coast Railway, the same company that built and managed the main London to Brighton route. The line opened in 1869, costing some £100,000. The journey took around ten minutes. The Kemp Town station, pictured here in 1961, stood in Coalbrook Road, which used to run between Freshfield Road and Sutherland Road.

Even for a branch line it was extremely short, at just over a mile in length. Yet it needed a huge amount of complex engineering to construct, including a fourteen-arch viaduct to carry it over Lewes Road (seen here coming down in 1976), a substantial three-arch bridge across Hartington Road, a tunnel 1,024 yards long, under Freshfield Road, and a massive excavation of chalk at the Kemp Town end.

A midway station on the line, off Lewes Road, at end of the Lewes Road viaduct, opened in 1873. This was reached by a covered walkway from the foot of the viaduct itself. Here, a church group (Lewes Road Congregational), all in their 'Sunday best', are about to depart for an outing in 1909. A halt, in the vicinity of Hartington Road, opened in January 1906. Despite all its facilities, the Kemp Town line failed. Passenger services were permanently withdrawn at the start of 1933. This saw the closure of Lewes Road station; Hartington Road Halt had already closed in 1911.

The Kemp Town line was then used for freight only, but operations were gradually wound down. The end came in 1971, when a special passenger train service operated for one day at hourly intervals. The train was the diesel locomotive seen here, as the track too weak to take a steam engine. Following closure, the site was bought by Brighton Council, who demolished the station, track and last remaining buildings. The site later became the Freshfield Industrial Estate. The southern end of the tunnel still exists.

Between 1901 and 1939, Brighton had an extensive tramway system that provided cheap and efficient transport on major thoroughfares throughout the town. Here, in 1902, the rails are being laid at Preston Circus, with Viaduct Road to the left, London Road in the centre, and New England Road to the right. Rails in London Road would be laid the following year.

Brighton's tram system eventually consisted of eight routes, lettered to denote the area covered – 'B' for Beaconsfield, 'N' for New England Road, etc. The 9-mile system was completed in 1904, with its depot in Lewes Road. Here, trams are seen outside the station in the 1930s, which, surprisingly, was the last route to open. This ran down Queen's Road, turned left at North Road, reached Grand Parade, then journeyed right to the Steine.

Trolleybuses, known just as trolleys, replaced the trams in 1939. They were first demonstrated going round the Level, and a town poll was held to determine the support they would get. Seen here is a view in Old Steine, taken on the day they started running. Trams still continued for a few more months before being finally withdrawn.

The last run of a Brighton trolleybus in 1961, photographed opposite the Level. Obviously only manoeuvrable to the limits of the connecting arms reaching the overhead power wires, the build-up of traffic in the 1950s, plus the increase in parking provision, made the buses difficult to run efficiently. They were withdrawn after serving the town for just twenty-two years.

The branch line to Kemp Town has already been detailed. It was also possible to get a train to Devil's Dyke, the popular beauty spot some 5½ miles north-east of the town. This opened in 1887 and operated for fifty-one years. Trains came off the main Brighton to Portsmouth line at Dyke Junction Halt, which was renamed Aldrington Halt in 1932. Then a winding track took passengers at little more than walking pace through open countryside to a station around 200 feet below the summit of the hill. This is seen here, around 1890, when the chalk cuttings hadn't become overgrown.

A later view of the station at the Dyke, around 1930, with visitors heading up to see the view and refresh themselves at one of several cafés and tea rooms. The line was obviously well patronised during the summer months, but proved unprofitable out of season. The Dyke railway closed in 1938. Today, much of the route survives as a cycle track.

One attraction at the Dyke was a cable railway spanning the Dyke chasm, installed in 1894. At sixpence a go, a cage-like car took four passengers across at a time, the ride lasting just a couple of minutes. It slowed at the centre, the highest point above ground (around 230 feet), and people often dropped lumps of chalk down to appreciate the height they were at. Although immensely popular with visitors, it lasted until around 1907. Today nothing remains except the weathered concrete bases for the two pylon towers either side of the chasm.

The cable railway was supplemented in 1897 by the Steep Grade Railway, seen here around 1905. This was on the northern slope of Dyke Hill, carrying visitors down to Poynings, some 700 feet below. It was a funicular railway – as one car went down, another was brought up – travelling at some 3 mph. At its steepest, the gradient was 1 in 1.5. Like the cable car ride, this lasted until around 1907 (the owner of the Dyke ran into financial problems) and was eventually dismantled. The base of the station building remains, and the 'scar,' where the track ran down the hill, also survives, which is best seen from the Poynings Road, below the Dyke area.

Returning to Brighton's seafront, another novelty ride for Victorian visitors was provided by Magnus Volk in 1896. This was officially the Brighton and Rottingdean Seashore Electric Railway, a carriage on stilt-like legs that took passengers from Black Rock to Rottingdean, through the waves via a seabed track way. The fare was 6d. It's seen here on opening day. In 1898, the railway carried its most famous passenger, the Prince of Wales, later Edward VII. He rode with the Duchess of Fife, his daughter, who lived at Kemp Town.

The carriage of the railway was soon nicknamed 'Daddy Long Legs' due to its spider-like appearance. The tram is seen here leaving the Rottingdean terminus pier in the late 1890s. The plant, generating the power for the line, was located below the pier. Sadly, this unique attraction only ran for four years. Brighton Corporation decided to extend the groynes between Black Rock and Rottingdean, so to continue the service the line would have to be diverted further out to sea, which would have made the ride more thrilling, but ultimately prove both too costly and impractical.
Volk's earlier electric railway (1883) still travels the seafront – the oldest railway of its kind in the world.

16

The Bedford Hotel

This book started with an amenity that was lost to a suspicious fire, and it ends with another. The original Bedford Hotel, pictured here in the 1950s, was opened in 1829, during a decade when many well-known buildings were erected. When monarchy abandoned the Pavilion, the Bedford is where members of the royal family stayed when visiting Brighton. Charles Dickens was a frequent guest. Fire ravaged the hotel in 1964, resulting in two deaths, but only the top two storeys were damaged. To everyone's surprise – and concern – the whole building was completely demolished and a new Bedford, clearly designed on graph paper, rose on the site in 1967. Another of Brighton's mystery fires; another fine building lost.

This book ends here, with the number of entries pushed to the limit. It would have been easy to continue with hundreds more examples of 'lost Brighton', including buildings not even touched on in the previous pages, such as military premises (Preston Barracks), municipal buildings (markets in the Old Town area), workhouses, hospitals, church halls, fire stations, plus other leisure and entertainment buildings – such as the tiny ice rink in Queen Square, recently demolished, seen here. Nothing stands still, old ways of doing things are gone, attitudes shift and change and tastes alter. But flick back through the pages of *Lost Brighton* and decide for yourself if the place really is better now than in the past. And consider why has so much changed, and so rapidly.